FRRLS-PT
310220
J 929.
Arment. Sac, David,
Important and famous
people /
$29.95

W9-AXW-801

No Lex 10/12

PEACHTREE CITY LIBRARY
201 WILLOWBEND ROAD
PEACHTREE CITY, GA 30269-1623

The Rourke Guide
to State Symbols

IMPORTANT AND FAMOUS PEOPLE

David and Patricia Armentrout

Rourke Publishing LLC
Vero Beach, Florida 32964

© 2002 Rourke Publishing LLC

All rights reserved. No part of this book may be reproduced or utilized in any form or by any means, electronic or mechanical including photocopying, recording, or by any information storage and retrieval system without permission in writing from the publisher.

www.rourkepublishing.com

PHOTO CREDITS:
©Hulton/Getty pages 8, 10, 14, 15, 30, 42
©Library of Congress pages 16, 44
©Office of the Governor of the State of Minnesota page 24 top
©Courtesy Gerald R. Ford Library page 27
©AP/wide world pages 17 top, 32 top
©Archive Photos all other photos

COVER ILLUSTRATION: Jim Spence

EDITORIAL SERVICES:
Pamela Schroeder

Library of Congress Cataloging-in-Publication Data

Armentrout, David and Patricia
    Important and famous people / David and Patricia Armentrout
        p. cm.— (The Rourke guide to state symbols)
    Includes index
    Summary: Briefly profiles one famous person associated with each of the fifty states, from Alabama's Rosa Parks through Wyoming's William Frederick "Buffalo Bill" Cody.
    ISBN 1-58952-086-6
    1. United States—Biography—Juvenile literature. [1. United States—Biography.] I. Armentrout, Patricia, 1960- II. Title. III. Series

CT217 .A55 2001
920.073—dc21   2001031977

Printed in the USA

TABLE OF CONTENTS

INTRODUCTION

Of all the people that have ever lived, how many became famous? How many were thought by others to be important? Since the dawn of time billions of people have walked the Earth. Very few are remembered by name. With so many people, what does someone have to do to become famous?

Most of the people we remember from history were leaders, or inventors, or explorers. Some are known for creating books or art. Maybe they were entertainers or great athletes. Some may be remembered for the terrible things they did.

Famous Americans have come from every state in the U.S. This book tells you a little about one famous person from each state. Many of the people you read about will be familiar to you. Some of them may not be so well known. Some people have become famous during their own lifetime, while others became famous after they died.

ALABAMA
Rosa Parks

    Rosa Parks was an ordinary citizen of Montgomery, Alabama. In 1955 Rosa refused to give up her bus seat to a white passenger. Back then, there were laws that treated black people unfairly. Rosa Parks was found guilty of breaking a law. Other African Americans in Alabama felt the way Rosa did. They did not ride city buses until things changed. Soon the United States Supreme Court changed the law that made it legal to separate blacks from whites.

ALASKA

Jack London

Jack London was not born in Alaska, but many of his stories were of Alaskan adventures. London traveled to Alaska in 1897. He spent years searching for gold in the Klondike. His experiences inspired many of his stories. His fans loved the way he wrote about life and death in the wilderness. *White Fang* and *Call of The Wild* are two of London's most popular books.

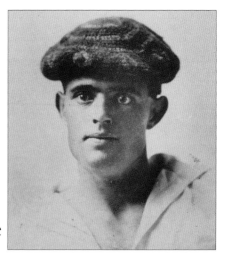

ARIZONA

Geronimo

Geronimo was an Apache Indian chief. The U.S. government forced the Apache to leave their home in Arizona and move to reservations in Florida and Alabama. Reservations are areas of land the government set aside for Native Americans to live on. For 10 years, Geronimo and his followers refused to be told where to live. They hid in the mountains. Geronimo finally surrendered. His tribe was forced to move—this time to Oklahoma. Geronimo died there in 1909.

ARKANSAS

William Jefferson Clinton

William Jefferson Clinton was born in 1946 in Arkansas. Bill Clinton was a good student. He studied law and became a lawyer. His greatest interest, however, was public service.

Bill Clinton became the attorney general and then governor of Arkansas. At age 32 he was the youngest person to become governor of Arkansas. His biggest accomplishment was becoming the 42nd President of the United States in 1992.

CALIFORNIA
George Lucas

If you don't know who George Lucas is, you most surely know of his work. George Lucas is a famous movie director, screen writer, and producer. Lucas was born in Modesto, California, in 1944. His first big success was the movie *American Graffiti*. He is best known for the *Star Wars* and *Indiana Jones* movies. His movies are among the most popular ever made.

COLORADO

Jack Dempsey

Boxing was not a popular or money-making sport until Jack Dempsey came along. Dempsey, born in Colorado in 1895, was a heavyweight boxer. His popularity brought attention and money to the sport of boxing. Out of 69 professional fights, Dempsey won 47 by knocking his opponent out. Dempsey died in 1983.

CONNECTICUT
Noah Webster

Noah Webster was a lexicographer. A lexicographer makes dictionaries. Webster was born in West Hartford, Connecticut, in 1758. He was a school teacher. He also served in the American Revolution. He started a daily newspaper and wrote several books. However, Webster is most famous for his dictionary. The *Webster Dictionary* lists thousands of words. It was the first dictionary to show differences between the American English language and British. Webster completed his dictionary in 1828.

DELAWARE
Henry Heimlich

    Heimlich became a household name when he invented the "Heimlich maneuver." Henry Heimlich, born in Delaware, invented the maneuver in 1974. The Heimlich maneuver is often used to save people who are choking. Hundreds of people have been saved by his discovery. Mr. Heimlich also invented other medical procedures and wrote a book.

FLORIDA

Janet Reno

The Attorney General is the highest ranking law officer in the United States. The job was never held by a woman until 1993. President Bill Clinton chose Janet Reno of Miami, Florida, to be the first woman attorney general. Reno was a lawyer and a state attorney general in Florida. Her experience convinced President Clinton she was the best person for the job. Janet Reno served as Attorney General of the United States for both terms of Bill Clinton's presidency.

GEORGIA
Martin Luther King, Jr.

    Martin Luther King, Jr., was born in Atlanta, Georgia. At age 17 he became a Baptist minister. He was a great leader in the struggle for civil rights. He believed in peaceful protest. Reverend King led marches and gave speeches. He believed that all people should have the same rights. He changed the way many people thought about civil rights. Sometimes his life was threatened by people who did not agree with him. On April 4, 1968, Martin Luther King, Jr., was shot and killed in Memphis, Tennessee.

HAWAII
Akebono

At 6 feet 9 inches (2 m) tall and 510 pounds (231 kg), Taro Akebono is a giant. He is also one of the best wrestlers in the ancient Japanese sport of Sumo wrestling. Sumo is one of the most popular sports in Japan. Akebono was born in Hawaii in 1969. He is the first foreign wrestler to reach the highest rank of Yokozuna, or Grand Champion. In fact, only two foreigners have made it to this rank. Both of them are from Hawaii.

IDAHO
Sacajawea

Lewis and Clark led a famous expedition across North America from 1804-1806. The expedition might have failed if it were not for Sacajawea. Sacajawea was a Shoshone Native American. She was born in Idaho around 1787. Sacajawea helped guide the expedition. She was able to get horses, food, and other supplies for Lewis and Clark. Some believe Sacajawea died in 1812. However, one story claims she lived until 1884.

ILLINOIS

Abraham Lincoln

Abraham Lincoln was the 16th President of the United States. Lincoln led the Union to victory in the American Civil War. Lincoln spoke out against slavery. It was during his Presidency that slavery was outlawed in the United States.

Because of his beliefs, Lincoln had many enemies. One of them was an actor named John Wilkes Booth. Booth shot Lincoln on April 14, 1865. Lincoln died the next day.

INDIANA

David Letterman

David Letterman has been called the "funniest man on television." He started his career as a weather forecaster at a television station in Indianapolis, Indiana. He went on to host two of the most popular late night shows of all time. His *Late Night with David Letterman* ran from 1982-1993. The *Late Show with David Letterman* started in 1993 and is still winning awards.

IOWA

Herbert Hoover

Becoming the President of the United States almost guarantees that you will be remembered. Herbert Hoover was the 31st President of the United States. His home state was Iowa. He was the President during a difficult time called the Great Depression. Although Hoover did everything he could to help the poor, he was blamed for not doing enough. He lost the next election to Franklin Roosevelt.

KANSAS

Amelia Earhart

There was a time when flying across the Atlantic Ocean was very dangerous. In 1932 Amelia Earhart lifted off in a small airplane. She was the first woman to fly alone across the Atlantic. The trip took 13 1/2 hours. She became famous around the world for her daring flight.

In 1937 Amelia Earhart and Edward Noonan set off to fly around the world. Their airplane disappeared somewhere over the Pacific Ocean and was never seen again.

KENTUCKY

Muhammad Ali

Ali was born in Louisville, Kentucky. He made a name for himself as one of the world's best boxers. Ali won the World Heavyweight Champion title three times. He was known for his colorful personality as well. He called himself "the greatest" and then went out and proved it. He liked to joke with the media. He once said he could "float like a butterfly and sting like a bee."

LOUISIANA

Louis Armstrong

Louis Armstrong was an American jazz musician. He was born in New Orleans, Louisiana, in 1900. He could sing and play the bugle, clarinet, and cornet. However, his favorite instrument was the trumpet. He was one of the greatest jazz trumpeters of all time. Louis recorded more than 1,500 songs in his lifetime. He also appeared in several movies and wrote a book about his life.

MAINE
Stephen King

Do you like to be scared? Some people enjoy watching horror movies or reading scary books. Stephen King must like to be scared. He's famous for writing scary books and short stories.

King learned to write at an early age. He wrote his first story when he was seven. His first published book was *Carrie*. More than 4 million copies were sold. *Carrie* was also made into a movie.

MARYLAND

Thurgood Marshall

Thurgood Marshall was born in Maryland in 1908. He was a lawyer and became famous fighting for civil rights. In 1939 he became one of the top lawyers in the country. He argued his cases in the highest court in America—the Supreme Court. He won 29 out of 32 court cases.

In 1967 Marshall was chosen as the first black member of the Supreme Court by President Johnson. He served as a Supreme Court Justice until he retired in 1991.

MASSACHUSETTS
John F. Kennedy

John F. Kennedy was born in Massachusetts in 1917. He became the 35th President of the United States in 1961. Kennedy was a hero before he became President. He was the commander of a navy torpedo boat in World War II. After his boat was rammed by a Japanese ship, he helped save the lives of several crewmen.

President Kennedy was killed by a gunman in 1963. His term as President was cut short, but he is remembered as one of our greatest leaders.

MICHIGAN
Charles Lindbergh

In 1927 it took 33 hours and 32 minutes for Charles Lindbergh to fly across the Atlantic Ocean. He flew alone from New York City to Paris, France, without stopping. The name of his plane was the "Spirit of St. Louis." He was the first person to make the flight across the Atlantic. Lindbergh was greeted as a hero in Europe and in the U.S.

MINNESOTA

Jesse Ventura

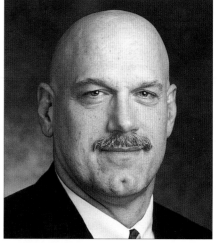

Politics and professional wrestling don't have much in common. However, Jesse Ventura combined his popularity in both areas. His strong desire to make a difference won him the title of governor of Minnesota in the 1998 election.

Ventura was born in Minneapolis in 1951. He served as a navy seal before his 11-year pro wrestling career. He moved on to politics in 1990. He was mayor of Brooklyn Park, Minnesota, until 1995.

MISSISSIPPI

Oprah Winfrey

Oprah Winfrey was born in Mississippi in 1954. She learned at an early age that she would have to work hard to succeed. Oprah moved to Nashville, Tennessee, at age 13 and later attended college. She became the first black woman to anchor the local Nashville news. Oprah began hosting a talk show in Chicago in 1984. People loved the show and it was soon shown all around the country. *The Oprah Winfrey Show* became one of the most popular programs on television.

MISSOURI
Walter Cronkite

Born in Saint Joseph, Missouri, Walter Cronkite became one of the best known journalists in the world. As a reporter he covered wars and presidential campaigns. He anchored the *CBS Evening News* for almost 20 years. To many people, he was like a trusted grandfather. He reported the news in a way that people understood. Cronkite retired from the evening news in 1981, but he continued working as a CBS News special reporter.

MONTANA

Jeannette Rankin

In the early years of our country, the state and federal governments were run by men. Women did not work in politics. Jeannette Rankin helped change that. In 1916 she became the first woman to be elected as a representative for the state of Montana. In fact, she was the first woman to be a member of the U.S. House of Representatives.

NEBRASKA
Gerald R. Ford

Gerald R. Ford was born in Omaha, Nebraska, in 1913. He later moved to Michigan where he studied law. Ford was elected to the U.S House of Representatives in 1948. He became the minority leader of the House in 1973. That year Ford was chosen by President Richard Nixon to be Vice President. He replaced Spiro Agnew who resigned. In 1974 Nixon resigned from the Presidency and Gerald Ford became the 38th president of the United States. Ford was the first President in U.S. history to serve as Vice President and President without ever being elected in a national election.

NEVADA

Andre Agassi

Andre Agassi is considered one of the best tennis players of all time. Andre was born in Las Vegas, Nevada, in 1970. When he was just a toddler his father taught him the game and became his trainer. As Andre grew older he practiced with many pro players. Andre Agassi became a professional tennis player in 1986. He won his first title the next year. Andre Agassi has won more than 40 singles titles in his career.

NEW HAMPSHIRE

Christa McAuliffe

Christa McAuliffe died in the explosion of the space shuttle Challenger in 1986. However, it is not her tragic death that she is remembered for.

Christa McAuliffe was a high school teacher in Concord, New Hampshire. She was chosen to be the first civilian in space. Her mission was to help bring excitement back to the space program.

New Jersey
Norman Schwarzkopf, Jr.

General Norman Schwarzkopf is better known as "Stormin' Norman." Schwarzkopf earned the rank of general in 1978. He was responsible for planning "Operation Desert Storm" in 1991 during the Persian Gulf War. The war freed the country of Kuwait after it was invaded by Iraq. Schwarzkopf wrote a book about his life after the Persian Gulf War. It is titled *It Doesn't Take a Hero*.

NEW MEXICO

William Hanna

Everyone loves cartoons. The talented people that work so hard to create them are artists. Many of the most popular cartoons came from the imagination of William Hanna. William Hanna was born in New Mexico in 1910. He and his partner Joseph Barbera created more than 2,000 cartoon characters. Among their most loved are Tom and Jerry, Yogi Bear, the Flintstones, the Smurfs, and Scooby-Doo.

NEW YORK

Susan B. Anthony

Susan B. Anthony was born in 1820. She is remembered for her fight for women's rights. She organized meetings and gave many speeches. She worked hard to change the New York state laws that discriminated against women. Anthony spent her life fighting for women's right to vote. Sadly, she died in 1906, before women were granted that right. The 19th Amendment to the Constitution granted women the right to vote in 1920.

NORTH CAROLINA

Dale Earnhardt

   As a boy, Dale Earnhardt watched his father race stock cars in North Carolina. Dale started racing as a teenager. He made it to the big time in 1975 when he was given the chance to race in the Winston Cup. For more than 25 years Earnhardt raced and won. He became one of the most successful race car drivers in the world. A crash at the 2001 Daytona 500 took the life of Dale Earnhardt.

NORTH DAKOTA

Theodore Roosevelt

   Theodore Roosevelt was the 26th President of the United States. He was one of the most popular Presidents in U.S. history. He lived much of his life in New York, but loved North Dakota.

   Roosevelt spent years ranching and hunting in the Dakota Territory. He was identified with the Wild West. Theodore Roosevelt National Park is in the western section of the state. His Elkhorn Ranch site can be visited there.

OHIO

Neil Armstrong

In July of 1969 an amazing thing happened. Man walked on the moon. American astronaut Neil Armstrong was the first person to step on the moon.

Armstrong was born in Wapakoneta, Ohio, in 1930. He started his career as a navy pilot in the Korean War. In 1962 he joined the astronaut training program. Seven years later he commanded the Apollo 11 lunar mission that took the astronauts to the moon.

OKLAHOMA

Garth Brooks

Country music has never been as popular as it is today. One reason is because of popular young country singers such as Garth Brooks. Brooks combines rock, pop, and traditional country sounds. He created his own style of country music. Garth Brooks became an immediate success in the country music field. He has won many awards for his songs and his fans love his live performances.

OREGON

Chief Joseph

Chief Joseph was a chief of the Nez Perce Indians in the Oregon Territory. The U.S. government tried to force the Nez Perce to move to Idaho. Chief Joseph, instead, led hundreds of Nez Perce toward Canada. The U.S. Army tried to stop him along the way. The Nez Perce fought back and defeated the soldiers. Later, an Army unit attacked the Nez Perce 30 miles (48 km) from the Canadian border. Five days later Chief Joseph surrendered. He and his people were sent to Oklahoma.

PENNSYLVANIA
Benjamin Franklin

Ben Franklin's story could fill an entire book. He was born in Boston, Massachusetts, but moved to Pennsylvania when he was a teenager. Franklin was an inventor, a printer, an author, a scientist, and a public servant. He also published and printed his own newspaper. He invented the Franklin stove and the lightning rod. He was chosen as the first Postmaster General of the U.S. Benjamin Franklin also helped write, and signed, the Declaration of Independence.

RHODE ISLAND

Oliver Hazard Perry

Perry's monument stands on a small island in Lake Erie. The monument was built as a peace memorial. It honors Oliver Hazard Perry and the men that fought in the Battle of Lake Erie. Perry was a naval commander born in Rhode Island in 1785. He joined the Navy at the early age of 14. Perry's defeat of the British Navy in the War of 1812 gave the American forces control of the area. He died of yellow fever at age 34.

SOUTH CAROLINA

Jesse Jackson

One of the best known civil rights leaders in modern times is Jesse Jackson. Jackson was born in Greenville, South Carolina, in 1941. As a college student, Jackson worked closely with Martin Luther King, Jr. In 1968 he became a Baptist minister. Reverend Jackson continued his fight for civil rights. In 1984 he tried to win the Democratic nomination for President. Jackson had many followers. However, he was not chosen as the Democratic candidate.

SOUTH DAKOTA

Sitting Bull

Tatanka Yotanka, or Sitting Bull, was a famous leader of the Sioux. As with many Native American tribes, the Sioux were forced by the U.S. government to leave their homelands. They were told they must live on reservations. Sitting Bull's warriors fought back. Sitting Bull is most famous for his battle against Colonel George Custer. Custer and all his men were killed in the battle. Sitting Bull later joined a Wild West Show with Buffalo Bill Cody.

TENNESSEE

Elvis Presley

Elvis Presley did not invent rock and roll, but he was one of its greatest performers. He was born in Mississippi, but soon moved to Memphis, Tennessee, where his musical career blossomed. Many of Presley's songs became instant hits. He was soon known as the "King" of rock and roll. After his death in 1977, his mansion, called Graceland, was made into a museum. It attracts thousands of fans each year.

TEXAS

George W. Bush

President George W. Bush started his job as the 43rd President of the United States in January of 2001. He won one of the closest elections in U.S. history. He is the son of George and Barbara Bush. His father was the 41st President of the United States.

George W. Bush served as a pilot for the Texas Air National Guard. He became the governor of Texas in 1994. He served as governor until his election to the Presidency.

UTAH

Brigham Young

Salt Lake City was founded by Brigham Young and the Mormon church in 1847. Young became the leader of the Mormon church after its founder Joseph Smith was killed. Young gathered nearly 5,000 members of the church and moved to the Great Salt Lake Valley. They settled there and built homes, churches, farms, and businesses. Today, Salt Lake City is the capital and the largest city in Utah.

VERMONT

George Dewey

George Dewey was born in Montpelier, Vermont. He became a hero of the Spanish American War. He attended the U.S. Naval Academy and graduated in 1858. He was promoted to commodore in the Navy. In 1898 the U.S. declared war on Spain. Commodore Dewey was asked to capture or destroy the Spanish naval fleet in Manila. Dewey's fleet attacked and completely destroyed the Spanish fleet, and not a single American sailor was killed.

VIRGINIA

Thomas Jefferson

Thomas Jefferson was born in Virginia in 1743. He was governor of Virginia, U.S. Minister to France, Secretary of State for George Washington, and Vice President to John Adams. He then served as President from 1801-1809.

Jefferson served Virginia and our country in many ways. However, he wanted to be remembered most for writing the Declaration of Independence.

WASHINGTON

Bill Gates

   Most people are familiar with computers at school, work, or at home. Bill Gates is known for his work in the computer world. He co-founded Microsoft in 1975. Microsoft makes all kinds of software for computers. Microsoft helped Gates become one of the world's best known businessmen and one of the richest people in the world. Bill Gates gives some of his wealth to charity and educational programs.

WEST VIRGINIA

Jonathan "Stonewall" Jackson

When Stonewall Jackson was born in 1824, West Virginia was still part of Virginia. Stonewall Jackson was an American soldier that fought for the Confederate army during the Civil War. He earned his nickname "Stonewall" during the Battle of Bull Run. It was said that his troops stood "like a stone wall" against the Union army. Jackson was accidentally shot and killed by his own men in 1863, the same year West Virginia became a state.

WISCONSIN

Harry Houdini

Harry Houdini was one of the world's most famous magicians. Houdini was born in Hungary, but his family moved to Wisconsin when he was a baby. Houdini performed many tricks. However, he was best known for his great escapes. One famous escape was performed in New York City. Houdini was tied with ropes and then locked inside a trunk. The trunk was wrapped with steel straps and then thrown into New York Harbor. Houdini escaped in less than 1 minute!

WYOMING

William Frederick Cody

The town of Cody, Wyoming, is named after William Cody. He earned the nickname Buffalo Bill after claiming he had killed 4,000 buffalo. He killed the buffalo to supply meat to railroad workers.

Cody founded a Wild West Show that traveled through Europe and the United States. The show starred himself, Native American leader Sitting Bull, and a sharpshooter named Annie Oakley.